PREPARE AND PAINT YOUR BACKGROUND

Mexican colours are vivid, going on for gaudy. Matt textures and chalky hues create the look.

Preparation can be minimal. Make sure surfaces are clean and non-greasy. Gloss finishes – paint or varnish – need sanding back with medium-grade sandpaper to provide a 'key' for the paint. No need to fill cracks and surface blemishes; these add character to a rustic painted piece. The pieces shown here were all painted with standard matt emulsion paints, intermixed for colour variation. Emulsion is the modern decorator's choice because it dries fast, is easy to apply, and provides an excellent surface for decoration. See below for ways of creating unusual effects with these standard paints, like the two-tone shades which imitate the patina of antique colour.

A CHARACTERISTICALLY MEXICAN EFFECT COMES FROM COMBINING STRONGLY SATURATED AND CONTRASTING COLOURS, AS SEEN HERE IN OUR ATTRACTIVE LATTICE WALL CUPBOARD, WHICH HAS BEEN PAINTED SHARP GREEN OUTSIDE AND BRIGHT PINK INSIDE.

THE RICH GLOW OF THE LIME GREEN FINISH ON OUR MEXICAN BENCH COMES FROM APPLYING A COAT OF SAP GREEN EMULSION ON TOP OF A CANARY YELLOW EMULSION. WHEN DRY THE GREEN COAT IS RUBBED DOWN CAREFULLY WITH DAMPENED MEDIUM-GRADE WET-AND-DRY PAPER, UNTIL THE YELLOW LAYER BEGINS TO SHOW THROUGH.

COLOURFUL AS A MEXICAN

South of the border, colour becomes as exciting as a firework display. Traditional Mexican embroideries with brilliant florals inspired many of the painted patterns shown in this vivid corner of a patio. What

traditional Mexican folk art teaches us is that the right clash of contrasting colours is wonderfully stimulating. Colours used here range from sharp pastels – lime green, cactus-flower pink, ochre yellow – to deep feisty

PONCHO

blues and reds, popular with peasant painters the world over. Patterns in this set include a stunning flower piece, shown here around a standard kitchen table, a charming pueblo street scene used to decorate a wooden blanket box, plus a clutch of lively border designs. As the results prove, the Mexican message where colours are concerned is not to be afraid of mixing it.

PAINTING WITH A PATTERN

Start with an undemanding border pattern to give yourself confidence and test out your tracing and brushwork.

Shown here are the steps involved in tracing off and painting the simple border motifs we arranged to enhance the side of a long wooden bench.

Points to remember: ● Use a hard lead pencil for the tracing down because this will give you a clear outline. ● Keep a clean copy of the tracing patterns – you might like to photocopy them a few times. You can then cut them up to fit awkward spaces without worrying about losing the originals. ● If you cut smaller pieces of transfer paper, be careful to leave yourself a big enough piece for the largest motif. ● Most of the patterns in this book were painted with fast-drying artist's acrylic colours, available in tubes from all artist's suppliers.

TRACING DOWN AND FILLING IN

You may find it easier to cut individual motifs from your pattern sheet, and cut smaller pieces of transfer paper.

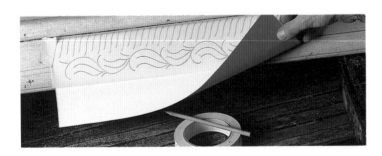

1 FIX PATTERN IN PLACE WITH MASKING TAPE. SLIP TRANSFER PAPER BENEATH.

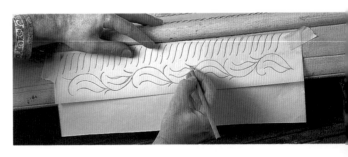

2 TRACE PATTERNS CAREFULLY AND FIRMLY WITH SHARP PENCIL.

5 ALTERNATE 'TADPOLE' SHAPES ARE BRUSHED IN WITH FINE BRUSH AND COLOUR A. START BRUSH STROKES AT THE TAPERING END, GRADUALLY INCREASING PRESSURE.

6 COLOUR A AND FINE BRUSH ARE USED AGAIN TO CREATE SWEEPING CURVES OF SECOND BORDER DESIGN. PAINT LARGER CURVES FIRST THEN ADD SMALLER LEAF SHAPES.

These dry with a matt finish, and are used thinned with a little water to 'single cream' consistency. Use an old plate as a palette. ● Use soft watercolour brushes in different sizes to paint motifs, including one fine one for outlining. There is no need to buy expensive sable brushes – synthetic bristles or mixed hair are fine.

MATERIALS CHECKLIST

WELL-SHARPENED HARD LEAD PENCIL, SCISSORS, MASKING TAPE, OLD PLATE, WATER JAR, KITCHEN PAPER OR TISSUES FOR WIPING BRUSHES, RULER OR TAPE FOR POSITIONING MOTIFS.

ACRYLIC COLOURS IN WHITE, ULTRAMARINE BLUE, CADMIUM RED, YELLOW OCHRE AND HOOKER'S GREEN.

TWO WATERCOLOUR BRUSHES, ONE FINE, ONE MEDIUM.

COLOUR RECIPES:

(A) ULTRAMARINE BLUE WITH TOUCH OF WHITE

(B) CADMIUM RED WITH TOUCH OF YELLOW OCHRE

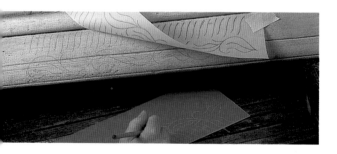

3 TRACED DOWN PATTERNS APPEAR CLEARLY ON PAINTED SURFACE.

4 WITH A SIMPLE WAVE DESIGN LIKE THIS YOU CAN DRAW AROUND A TEMPLATE FOR SPEED. MAKE YOUR OWN TEMPLATE BY TRACING OFF THE 'WAVE' BORDER ONTO CARD.

7 COLOUR A AND MEDIUM BRUSH ARE USED TO COLOUR IN 'WAVE' DESIGN, OUTLINED WITH TEMPLATE. USE FREE HAND TO STEADY PAINTING HAND AND BRUSH.

8 A CLEAN FINE BRUSH AND COLOUR B ARE USED TO BRING THE WHOLE BORDER TO LIFE WITH FLASHES OF CHILLI RED.

1 USE FREE HAND TO STEADY PAINTING HAND AS YOU BRUSH IN WHITE 'EYE' SHAPES WITH COLOUR A. DON'T WORRY ABOUT LOOSENESS IN EXECUTION.

2 SIZE OF BRUSH DETERMINES THICKNESS OF STROKE. A FINER BRUSH IS USED TO ADD SLENDER LEAF SHAPES.

2 DOUBLING UP ONE MOTIF CREATES A TWO-STOREY COLONNADED BUILDING. REMEMBER A SHARP PENCIL HELPS GREATLY IN TRACING OFF MOTIFS CLEARLY.

3 USING COLOURS C, D AND E AND MEDIUM BRUSH, COLOUR IN BASIC FOLIAGE AND BUILDING SHAPES.

COLOUR RECIPES

(A) WHITE WITH TOUCH OF CADMIUM RED
(B) CADMIUM RED
(C) WHITE
(D) YELLOW OCHRE WITH A LITTLE WHITE
(E) HOOKER'S GREEN WITH TOUCH OF WHITE AND YELLOW OCHRE
(F) 2 PARTS CADMIUM RED, 1 PART YELLOW OCHRE
(G) HOOKER'S GREEN

BORDERLINE BRILLIANCE

*Simple borders made up of two or three colours are fun to do and look
excitingly rich in these two Mexican designs.*

3 COLOUR B IS USED TO DASH IN SQUIGGLES AND
CROSS-HATCHING.

1 BUILDING BLOCK SYSTEM IS USED TO CREATE PUEBLO
STREET SCENE FROM A FEW BASIC ELEMENTS. USE IDEAS
HERE AS INSPIRATION.

4 USE SINGLE BRUSH STROKE TO MAKE TREE TRUNKS.
SWITCH TO FINE BRUSH AND COLOUR F TO ADD FINER
BUILDING DETAILS.

5 IMPROVISED DETAILING AS SHOWN HERE CAN ADD
IMPACT TO YOUR PAINTED DESIGNS. THERE IS NO NEED
TO BE TOO ELABORATE. TREE SHAPES ARE SIMPLY SHADED
WITH COLOUR G.

AUTHOR'S TIP Don't be afraid to improvise by adding to, or juggling with, basic
patterns. Practise alternatives first on paper so you don't lose spontaneity.

1 TRACED DOWN PAPER PATTERN FOR THE MEXICAN FLOWER PIECE SHOWING THE BLUE LINE TO FOLLOW FOR PAINTING ON THE GREEN TABLE. NOTE: THE MAIN ROSE MOTIF DETAILS ARE PAINTED OVER THE FIRST COLOUR LAYER. EITHER RE-TRACE THE DETAILS OR USE THE TRACING AS A GUIDE TO PAINT THEM FREEHAND.

4 COLOUR C IS USED TO FILL IN SMALL FLOWER SHAPES WHICH ARE THEN HIGHLIGHTED WITH COLOUR D.

5 WHITE HIGHLIGHTS (COLOUR D) ADD TYPICAL FOLKSY CONTRAST. USE A FINE BRUSH AND PRACTISE A LITTLE ON PAPER FIRST TO ACHIEVE FLUENT BUT DELICATE STROKES.

AUTHOR'S TIPS As it is invariably easier to paint designs on a horizontal surface, on tricky shapes try turning the piece, and tip furniture on its side as necessary. Also, most painting of this sort has a 'direction', so always orient yourself appropriately.

Having cut your teeth on the simpler patterns, it is time to have fun with colour and the exuberant floral motifs which make such a stunning addition to your painted furniture.

2 COLOUR A IS USED TO FILL IN THE RED ROSE AND PAIR OF BUDS. USE A MEDIUM BRUSH.

3 USING COLOUR B FILL IN GREEN LEAF SHAPES AND CALYXES.

6 FINISHING TOUCHES: A YELLOW CENTRE (COLOUR E) AND DARKER SHADING (COLOUR F) MAKE THE ROSE MORE VIVID STILL, PLUS LIGHTER GREEN (COLOUR G) HIGHLIGHTS LEAVES.

7 THIS DETAIL SHOWS HOW THE FLORAL DESIGN CAN EASILY BE EXPANDED. TO EXTEND ON THE OTHER SIDE, FLIP THE TRACING OVER.

COLOUR RECIPES

(A) CADMIUM RED

(B) HOOKER'S GREEN

(C) WHITE WITH TOUCH OF ULTRAMARINE BLUE

(D) WHITE

(E) YELLOW OCHRE

(F) CADMIUM RED WITH TOUCH OF ULTRAMARINE BLUE

(G) HOOKER'S GREEN WITH TOUCH OF YELLOW OCHRE AND WHITE

PUNCHY DETAILS RAISE THE COLOUR TEMPERATURE

Hot sunny colours sing out against a deep blue background colour. Simple shapes are completely transformed by our Mexican designs.

A POSSE OF PATTERN. IT DOES NOT NEED A LOT OF PAINT TO TRANSFORM SMALLER ITEMS LIKE THE PRETTY DECORATIVE CAGES AND BOTTLE BASKET SHOWN HERE. NOTE HOW DIFFERENT THE 'TADPOLE' BORDER LOOKS EXECUTED IN DIFFERENT COLOURWAYS.

THE SAME SHAPE CAN BE ADAPTED TO FIT QUITE DIFFERENT DECORATIVE NEEDS. HERE, FOR INSTANCE, SLENDER LEAF SHAPES AND BERRIES ADDED END-TO-END MAKE A LIVELY LINEAR DECORATION FOR THE BACK OF THE MEXICAN CHAIR.

CONTRAST PANELS BREAK UP THE SURFACE OF THE LIME GREEN BENCH AND ALSO PROVIDE AN OPPORTUNITY FOR MORE RIOTOUS COLOUR, USING THE 'TADPOLE' BORDER IN DIFFERENT COLOURWAYS. CONTRAST PANELS FRAMED WITH BORDERS ARE AN IDEAL WAY TO LIVEN UP LARGE PLAIN SURFACES.

IMPROMPTU PLACE MATS IN THE LIGHTER, BRIGHTER MEXICAN HUES DECORATE A SCRUBBED SYCAMORE TABLE TOP. NOTICE HOW THE 'TADPOLE' BORDER OUTSIDE THE PANEL TURNS INTO AN AMUSING DECORATIVE FRINGE. THE TEMPLATE COMES IN USEFUL AGAIN TO ADD A PINK RICK-RACK TRIM AROUND THE TABLE BASE. IN THE SAME INSOUCIANT SPIRIT, BANGLES OF BRILLIANT COLOUR HIGHLIGHT THE TABLE LEGS.

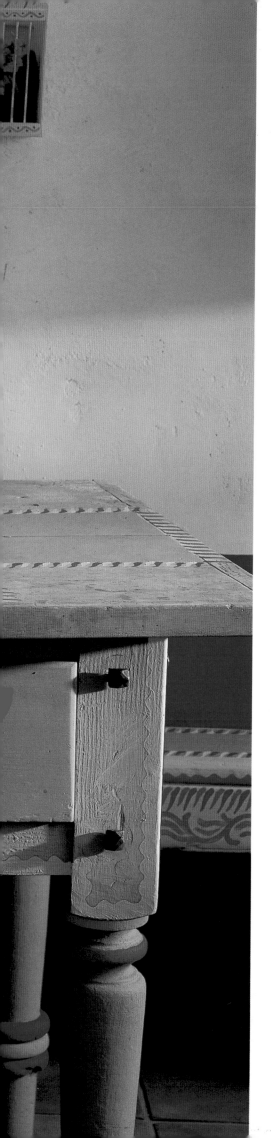

Colour works cumulatively in a setting as piquant as *salsa cruda*. If you use enough colours of the same value, the final effect is surprisingly convincing.

A FEW SQUIGGLES ARE ALL THAT IS NEEDED TO GIVE THIS TERRACOTTA POT AND PLANT HOLDER THE TRUE ACAPULCO FLAVOUR. TRY THIS SORT OF FREEHAND DECORATION AFTER YOU HAVE EXPERIMENTED WITH THE OTHER PATTERNS. YOU WILL FIND IT JUST FLOWS NATURALLY OFF YOUR BRUSH.